Words For A Wounded World

I have had the privilege of knowing Mark for several years, and one quality shines above all the rest—his deep passion for Christ. He is a man who not only believes in the transforming power of God's Word but lives it out with discipline, humility, and conviction. That same passion and faith flow richly through the pages of Words for a Wounded World.

This collection of Scripture-inspired poems is not just words on a page; it is an invitation to draw closer to the heart of God. Each poem serves as a pathway—guiding you into deeper faith, fortifying your spirit, and reminding you of God's unshakable love. As you read, take your time, linger in the truth, and allow the Spirit to minister to your soul.

I believe this book will stand the test of time and become a source of encouragement and substance for many. It is a work that points people back to Christ, and in that way, it carries eternal value.
--**Paige Michael Williams**, Teaching Pastor, *Intersection Church,* Prophet, Author of *Lessons from Heaven, The Disciples Manual,* and *Prayer, Mysteries, and Relationship*

***

Accessible, biblical, and richly spiritual, Mark Richard's poems bridge art and theology. With hymn-like cadence and gospel-centered focus, Words for a Wounded World can inspire worship, fuel evangelism, and even serve as a teaching tool.

--**Martins Jayeoba**, Ph.D., Educationist, Editor at *Kharis Publishing, IL*

WORDS FOR A WOUNDED WORLD

Scriptural Poems of Truth
and Hope to Awaken,
Convict, and Heal

Mark Richard

Published by KHARIS PUBLISHING, an imprint of
KHARIS MEDIA LLC.

Copyright © 2025 Mark Richard

ISBN-13: 978-1-63746-564-6

ISBN-10: 1-63746-564-5

Library of Congress Control Number:

Unless otherwise noted, all Scripture quotations are taken
from the New King James Version® (NKJV). Copyright ©
1982 by Thomas Nelson. Used by permission.

This work is intended to edify the body of Christ by
equipping believers to walk in truth and righteousness by
the Word of God.

All KHARIS PUBLISHING products are available at
special quantity discounts for bulk purchases for sales
promotions, premiums, fund-raising, and educational
needs. For details, contact:

Kharis Media LLC
Tel: 1-630-909-3405
support@kharispublishing.com
www.kharispublishing.com

To all those who pick up this book, may God's Word presented herein be deeply revealed to you as it was and is to me.

CONTENTS

PREFACE

It started with Tucker.

A young husband and father, Tucker was quietly losing a war few could see, caught in the grip of pornography. He wanted to break free, but didn't know how. As I ministered to him, the Holy Spirit stirred something unexpected in my heart: to write him a poem—a poem that would speak Truth and Scripture to the soul.

I called it *Lured: The War for Your Soul*. It wasn't just creative expression—it was warfare. Each line of the poem was grounded in Scripture, calling Tucker to recognize the spiritual battle he faced, the enemy's deception, and the power of God's Truth. I gave it to him along with verses that the poem was designed to teach, and questions for reflection.

Weeks later, he told me that the poem and the Scriptures that followed became his lifeline. He kept them with him. He read them in moments of temptation. And most importantly, they reminded him of the Truth—that he was not alone, and that freedom was possible through Christ.

Since Tucker, I've been inspired to write more poems saturated in scripture for many whom I've ministered to.

Then there was Char.

Battling chronic illness and emotional discouragement, Char found strength in another poem I had written: *Thanks Be to God!* She began reading it aloud daily. The

Scriptures that followed helped saturate her mind with God's Truth. She told me that her perspective—and even her physical symptoms—began to shift. She felt lighter, closer to God, more hopeful. She was being renewed in both spirit and body.

These are just two of many. And they are the reason for this book.

WHY I WROTE THIS BOOK

Each poem you'll find here was born from a specific moment of ministry—crafted for someone I was walking alongside, praying for, or ministering to. They flowed from my time in prayer, the Word, and meditating on the Truth as well as from the prompting of the Holy Spirit.

Poems for: an atheist family member, a weary and heavy burdened sister in Christ, my brothers at church who needed encouragement to keep in prayer, a new believer who needed to know the transformative power of God's Word, a lonely widow, a lukewarm Christian, a believer friend who has difficulties in relationships, a person struggling with sexual identity, a religious family member who goes to church but doesn't know Jesus, a person who says there's no hell, and many more.

As I witnessed the fruit of healing, conviction, and encouragement, I sensed God calling me to share these poems more broadly. What began as a personal ministry has now become a devotional offering for you.

Because we are all living on borrowed time, none of us knows the day, the hour, or the moment we'll stand before our Creator. That's why we must seek the Lord while He may be found. Tomorrow is not promised. These poems get you in the Word and closer to its author.

May these poems stir your heart to repentance. May they anchor your mind in Truth. May they point you to the healing, saving power of Jesus Christ.

WHO THIS BOOK IS FOR

Whether you're a long-time believer, a new follower of Jesus or someone seeking to know Him more deeply, this book is for you. Whether you're strong in the Word or just starting to study it, you will find something here to challenge, comfort, and transform you.

Perfect for individual or group study, these poems, Scriptures, and reflection questions and devotional prompts are a great way to dive deeper than ever before into God's Word.

MORE THAN A BOOK OF POEMS: A THREE-PART EXPERIENCE

Inside *Words for a Wounded World*, you'll encounter:

- **16 Scripture-Inspired Poems**, each a poetic distillation of biblical truth—encouraging, convicting, and Christ-exalting.

- **More than 250 NKJV Scriptures** carefully selected and listed after each poem, grounding every word in the eternal Word of God.

- **Reflection Questions and Devotional Prompts** to help you not just read—but respond. These are designed to engage the heart, stir spiritual conviction, and lead the reader into a deeper walk with the Lord. These include:

  - **Heart Questions** – to provoke deeper reflection

  - **Action Steps** – to put truth into practice

  - **Prayer Prompts** – to guide your time with the Lord

  - **Journaling Space** – to record what God is speaking to you

This Three-Part Structure Makes the Book Ideal For:

- Individual devotion

- Small group studies

- Prayer circles

- Counseling or discipleship ministries

- Gift-giving to those in spiritual need

Readers Have Said

"These poems are a God-send. I am so privileged to read them. They keep my mind on Christ, especially when life feels chaotic."

"These beautiful poems speak life and are teaching my family and me Scriptures, too."

"I keep these poems at my desk and in my car. I read them when I need to remember what's true as I face life's many challenges."

"This isn't a one-and-done collection of poems. I am drawn to reread the poems over and over again. My family and I love the guided questions and prayers."

You're invited into a journey. A journey through poetry, but more importantly, through the timeless Truth of God's Word. Let each poem minister to you. Let the Scriptures transform you. Let the questions draw you closer to God.

And may you find, in every page, a healing Word for your wounded world.

PART I:
FOUNDATIONS OF GOD, TRUTH, AND SALVATION

1

FROM FIG LEAVES TO WHITE ROBES

A telling of man's fall and redemption
through Christ

BY MARK RICHARD

In Eden's light, where peace once reigned,
Man walked with God, untouched by shame.
From every tree his hand could eat—
Save one: the fruit of death, deceit.

The Lord had warned with a holy voice,
"Eat not this tree, nor make that choice.
For in that day, if you defy,
You shall indeed, and surely, die."

But sin slithered in through the serpent's guile,
Twisting God's Truth with a cunning smile.
"Did God say so? You shall not surely die—
You'll be like Him, and your eyes will rise."

The woman gazed, the fruit was fair,
Desire burned, rebellion snared.

She took; she ate, and gave to man—
And thus on man the curse began.

Their eyes were opened, and shame rushed in,
Their innocence now exchanged for sin.
They stitched up fig leaves trying to hide,
But still God walked—yes, He arrived.

"Where are you, Adam?" came God's call,
His voice rang through Eden's fall.
"I heard, I feared, for I was bare."
Sin bred distance, shame, despair.

"Have you eaten?" God inquired.
Then blame passed on as fear transpired.
The woman blamed the serpent's tongue,
With Eden's harmony further undone.

To dust the man would now return,
The ground would fight, the thorns would burn.
The woman, too, would bear in pain,
And man would rule in toil and strain.

But oh, behold—amid the blame,
God whispered forth a glorious name:
"The Seed shall come, and crush the head
Of him who lured your souls to dread."

And there—a sign of mercy shone:
God clothed their shame with blood alone.
An animal slain, a life laid bare—
The first red stain, salvation's glare.

Banished then from Eden's gate,
Guarded by sword, sealed by fate.
But even in exile, hope was sown—
A scarlet thread from throne to throne.

For through one man, death spread to all,
A world in chains since Adam's fall.
Yet through one Man, so pure, so true,
The gift of grace would flow anew.

He came—God's Son, the spotless Lamb,
To bear our guilt; fulfill God's plan.
He took our shame, our sin, our stain,
That to live is Christ and to die is gain.

For as in Adam all must die,
In Christ we're raised to life on high.
From fig leaves sown in fear and blame,
To robes of white in Jesus' name.

So let us not forget the cost,
The garden gained, the garden lost.
Yet greater still—the love outpoured,
The grace of Christ, our risen Lord.

POEM BASED ON THESE SCRIPTURES

All Scripture references are from the New King James Version (NKJV).

Genesis 2:16–17

And the Lord God commanded the man, saying, "Of every tree of the garden you may freely eat; but of the tree of the knowledge of good and evil you shall not eat, for in the day that you eat of it you shall surely die."

Genesis 3:1, 4-6

Now the serpent was more cunning than any beast of the field which the Lord God had made. And he said to the woman, "Has God indeed said, 'You shall not eat of every tree of the garden'?" Then the serpent said to the woman, "You will not surely die. For God knows that in the day you eat of it your eyes will be opened, and you will be like God, knowing good and evil."

So, when the woman saw that the tree was good for food, that it was pleasant to the eyes, and a tree desirable to make one wise, she took of its fruit and ate. She also gave to her husband with her, and he ate.

Genesis 3:7, 9–13

Then the eyes of both of them were opened, and they knew that they were naked; and they sewed fig leaves together and made themselves coverings. Then the Lord God called to Adam and said to him, "Where are you?"

So he said, "I heard Your voice in the garden, and I was afraid because I was naked; and I hid myself."

And He said, "Who told you that you were naked? Have you eaten from the tree…?"

Then the man said, "The woman whom You gave to be with me, she gave me of the tree, and I ate."

The woman said, "The serpent deceived me, and I ate."

Genesis 3:14–19

So the Lord God said to the serpent: "Because you have done this… On your belly you shall go… And I will put enmity between you and the woman, and between your seed and her Seed; He shall bruise your head, and you shall bruise His heel."

To the woman He said: "I will greatly multiply your sorrow…"

Then to Adam He said… "Cursed is the ground for your sake… For dust you are, and to dust you shall return."

Genesis 3:21

Also for Adam and his wife the Lord God made tunics of skin, and clothed them.

Genesis 3:22–24

The Lord God sent him out of the Garden of Eden… So He drove out the man; and He placed cherubim… to guard the way to the tree of life.

Romans 5:12

Therefore, just as through one man sin entered the world, and death through sin, and thus death spread to all men, because all sinned—

I Timothy 2:14

And Adam was not deceived, but the woman being deceived, fell into transgression.

Romans 5:15–19

Much more the grace of God and the gift by the grace of the one Man, Jesus Christ, abounded to many… even so through one Man's righteous act the free gift came to all men… by one Man's obedience many will be made righteous.

Philippians 1:21
For to me, to live is Christ, and to die is gain.

I Corinthians 15:21–22
For since by man came death, by Man also came the resurrection of the dead.
For as in Adam all die, even so in Christ all shall be made alive.

REFLECTION & DEVOTIONAL PROMPTS

Heart Questions

Reflect prayerfully on these soul-searching questions:

- Where in your life are you tempted to cover yourself with "fig leaves" rather than bring your sin, shame, or fear to the Lord?

- How do you respond when God calls out, "Where are you?" in seasons of sin or hiding?

- What does the promise of redemption through Christ mean to you personally?

- How do you see God's mercy even in His judgment in the Genesis account?

- Are you living more as one in Adam—defined by sin and shame—or one in Christ—clothed in grace and righteousness?

Action Steps

Live out the truth in practical, Spirit-led ways:

- Confess any areas where you've been hiding from God. Name them, and surrender them to Christ. (1 John 1:9)

- Receive the truth that you are no longer clothed in shame, but robed in Christ's righteousness. Declare it out loud! (Isaiah 61:10)

- Study Romans 5 this week and highlight the contrasts between Adam and Christ.

- Extend grace to someone who is struggling under shame. Share this poem and offer to pray with them.

- Meditate on the power of Genesis 3:15 – God's first promise of the Savior – and let it anchor your hope.

Prayer Prompts

Use these to guide your time of communion with God:

- Lord, thank You that even in my rebellion, You pursue me. You do not leave me in shame, but lovingly call me back to Yourself.

- Jesus, I believe You are the promised Seed who crushed the serpent's head. Thank You for clothing me in Your righteousness.

- Father, help me to stop blaming others or hiding in fear. I want to walk in the light, clothed in truth and grace.

- Holy Spirit, show me where I'm still living under the curse instead of the cross. Lead me into freedom.

Journaling Space

Write from the heart:

- What is the Holy Spirit revealing to you?

- What emotions did this poem stir in you?

- What area of guilt or shame are you ready to surrender today?

- How has Christ redeemed something broken in your life?

- What do you sense God is saying to you through this time of reflection?

From fig leaves sown in fear and blame,
To robes of white in Jesus' name.

Let this be your testimony today.

2

CHRIST, OUR LIVING WORD

A poem about the eternal, powerful,
sanctifying Word made flesh—
Jesus Christ

BY MARK RICHARD

Before the dawn of time began,
The Word was there—God's perfect plan.
Not ink on scroll or sound in air,
But Christ Himself, the Word made bare.
"In the beginning," life took flight,
And through the Word came Truth and Light.

The Word of God is not asleep—
It pierces hearts, as it cuts down deep.
Alive, it speaks with holy flame,
Convicting, cleansing, all intents in vain.
Sharper than a sword it stands,
Discerning thoughts with nail-scarred hands.

It does not falter, fade, or fail—
It always goes forth to prevail.
It breaks the chains, renews the mind,
And leaves the lies of flesh behind.
It sanctifies the soul with grace,
And leads us to the Savior's face.

O Word of Truth, how firm you stand,
A light to guide, a Sword in hand.
You teach, correct, and train in right,
You turn the dark to morning light.
From age to age, Your voice is heard—
Eternal, living, breathing Word.

Your Word, O Lord, I hide within,
To guard my heart from every sin.
It is my shield, my strength, my stay,
My compass when I lose my way.
It washes clean like holy rain,
Restoring joy and healing pain.

Through You we are reborn anew—
Old things are gone; all things made true.
Your Spirit shapes us in Your mold,
From glory unto glory bold.
As we behold You face to face,
We're changed by mercy, love, and grace.

O Word who walked the earth below,
To save the lost, to make God known—
We love You, Lord, and keep Your ways,
You dwell within and light our days.
Your truth has made us sanctified—
Forever Yours, now crucified.

So let the world speak fables loud,
We stand on Scripture, strong and proud.
No trend or myth can override
The Truth in which Your saints abide.
For every word You've ever said
Is life and light, our daily bread.

POEM BASED ON THESE SCRIPTURES

All Scripture references are from the New King James Version (NKJV).

John 1:1–5
In the beginning was the Word, and the Word was with God, and the Word was God... All things were made through Him... In Him was life, and the life was the light of men...

John 1:14
And the Word became flesh and dwelt among us, and we beheld His glory... full of grace and truth.

Hebrews 4:12–13
For the word of God is living and powerful... piercing... a discerner of the thoughts and intents of the heart...

Isaiah 55:11
So shall My word be... it shall not return to Me void... it shall prosper in the thing for which I sent it.

Isaiah 40:8
The grass withers, the flower fades, But the word of our God stands forever.

Romans 12:2
Do not be conformed to this world, but be transformed by the renewing of your mind…

John 17:17
Sanctify them by Your truth. Your word is truth.

II Timothy 3:16
All Scripture is given by inspiration of God… profitable for doctrine, for reproof, for correction…

Psalm 119:105
Your word is a lamp to my feet and a light to my path.

Psalm 119:11
Your word I have hidden in my heart, that I might not sin against You.

Ephesians 5:26
…that He might sanctify and cleanse her with the washing of water by the word.

I Peter 1:23
…having been born again… through the word of God which lives and abides forever.

II Corinthians 5:17
If anyone is in Christ, he is a new creation… all things have become new.

II Corinthians 3:18

...we all... beholding... the glory of the Lord, are being transformed... from glory to glory...

John 14:21

He who has My commandments and keeps them, it is he who loves Me...

John 14:23–24

If anyone loves Me, he will keep My word... We will come to him and make Our home with him...

Psalm 119:160

The entirety of Your word is truth, and every one of Your righteous judgments endures forever.

Matthew 4:4

Man shall not live by bread alone, but by every word that proceeds from the mouth of God.

II Peter 1:20

No prophecy of Scripture is of any private interpretation.

I Corinthians 14:24

...an unbeliever... is convinced by all, he is convicted by all.

REFLECTION & DEVOTIONAL PROMPTS

Heart Questions

- Do you truly treasure the Word of God as your daily bread, or has it become something secondary in your life?

- In what ways has God's Word changed your thinking, your habits, and your identity?

- Are you hiding the Word in your heart, or are you relying on surface-level devotion?

- How would your life look different if you treated Scripture as alive, sharp, and holy?

- Do you love Jesus by keeping His Word (John 14:23), or are there areas of compromise and disobedience?

Action Steps

- Set a fresh intention to read and meditate on Scripture daily—even just one Psalm or a Gospel passage each morning.

- Memorize one verse this week from the poem's Scripture list—start with Psalm 119:105 or Hebrews 4:12.

- Renew your mind this week with Romans 12:2. Identify one lie you've believed and replace it with biblical truth.

- Declare aloud: "God's Word is alive in me. It changes how I think, how I speak, and how I live."

- Reflect on John 1 and write down what it means to you that Jesus is the Word made flesh.

Prayer Prompts

- Lord Jesus, You are the Living Word—alive, active, and eternal. Let me never grow dull to Your voice.

- Father, help me to love Your Word as treasure, not as task. Give me fresh hunger and joy when I open Scripture.

- Holy Spirit, pierce my heart through the Word. Convict me, renew me, and sanctify me in truth.

- God, write Your Word on my heart. Let it be my light, my sword, and my strength in every season.

Journaling Space

Use this space to reflect and write from the heart:

- What specific verse in this poem or Scripture list spoke to you most deeply?

- Where is God calling you to let the Word "cut" and correct?

- How have you seen God's Word renew your thinking or restore your heart?

- Write a personal declaration of what the Word of God means to you.

So let the world speak fables loud,
We stand on Scripture, strong and proud.

3

CREATED FOR HIS GLORY

A tapestry of truth about your
identity, calling, and hope

BY MARK RICHARD

Before time began, He fashioned a plan,
With purpose divine for woman and man.
In His own image, He formed us with care—
Each breath a reminder: God placed us there.

"I am fearfully, wonderfully made!" we declare,
Marvelous works, beyond all compare.
His thoughts toward us are peace, not despair—
A future, a hope, His love laid bare.

Not random, not worthless, not born of chance,
But chosen in Christ before life's first glance.
Created in Jesus for good works to do,
He set them in place, and He'll carry us through.

He made us for glory—His own, not ours,
To shine like the stars, transformed by His powers.

To love Him with heart, soul, strength, and mind,
And love every neighbor with mercy, be kind.

He calls us to justice, to walk humbly near,
To live in His presence and follow in fear.
To study the Scriptures, rightly divide,
And be doers of Truth with nothing to hide.

Rejoice in the Lord—let thanksgiving flow,
Pray without ceasing wherever you go.
Whether eating or drinking, let all that you do
Be done for His glory—faithful and true.

Go into the world—make disciples, proclaim
The Gospel of Christ, the power of His Name.
Baptize and teach them all He commands,
And know that He's with us with nail-scarred hands.

Don't grow weary when the days are long,
For in due season we'll reap if we're strong.
Bear with each other, lift burdens in grace,
As fellow believers we run this race.

And when our works rise before heaven's throne,
Each secret revealed, each motive made known—
Our reward won't be silver, or treasures that rust,
But joy in His presence, in Jesus we trust.

For eye hasn't seen, and ear hasn't heard,
The splendor prepared for those who've preferred
To follow the Savior, to trust and obey—
Our purpose fulfilled at the dawn of that Day.

POEM BASED ON THESE SCRIPTURES

All Scripture references are from the New King James Version (NKJV).

II Timothy 1:9
...who has saved us and called us with a holy calling, not according to our works, but according to His own purpose and grace which was given to us in Christ Jesus before time began,

Genesis 1:27
So God created man in His own image; in the image of God He created him; male and female He created them.

Psalms 139:14
I will praise You, for I am fearfully and wonderfully made; Marvelous are Your works, And that my soul knows very well.

Jeremiah 29:11
"For I know the thoughts that I think toward you," says the Lord, "thoughts of peace and not of evil, to give you a future and a hope."

Ephesians 2:10
For we are His workmanship, created in Christ Jesus for good works, which God prepared beforehand that we should walk in them.

Isaiah 43:7

Everyone who is called by My name, Whom I have created for My glory; I have formed him, yes, I have made him.

Colossians 1:16

For by Him all things were created that are in heaven and that are on earth… All things were created through Him and for Him.

Mark 12:30–31

'And you shall love the Lord your God with all your heart, with all your soul, with all your mind, and with all your strength.' … 'You shall love your neighbor as yourself.'

Micah 6:8

He has shown you, O man, what is good; And what does the Lord require of you But to do justly, To love mercy, And to walk humbly with your God?

II Timothy 2:15

Be diligent to present yourself approved to God, a worker who does not need to be ashamed, rightly dividing the word of truth.

James 1:22

But be doers of the word, and not hearers only, deceiving yourselves.

I Thessalonians 5:16–18

Rejoice always, pray without ceasing, in everything give thanks; for this is the will of God in Christ Jesus for you.

I Corinthians 10:31

Therefore, whether you eat or drink, or whatever you do, do all to the glory of God.

Matthew 28:19–20

Go therefore and make disciples of all the nations... teaching them to observe all things that I have commanded you; and lo, I am with you always...

Galatians 6:9

And let us not grow weary while doing good, for in due season we shall reap if we do not lose heart.

Ecclesiastes 12:13–14

Fear God and keep His commandments, For this is man's all. For God will bring every work into judgment...

I Corinthians 2:9

Eye has not seen, nor ear heard... the things which God has prepared for those who love Him.

REFLECTION & DEVOTIONAL PROMPTS

Heart Questions

- Do you believe that your life was designed with eternal purpose, or do you struggle with feelings of insignificance or confusion?

- What does it mean to you personally to be "created for His glory"?

- Are there any "good works" God has prepared for you that you've been avoiding or delaying?

- How well are you living out the greatest commandments: To love God fully and love your neighbor sacrificially?

- In what ways are you preparing for that final day when your life will be revealed before God's throne?

Action Steps

- Affirm your identity in Christ by meditating on Isaiah 43:7 and Ephesians 2:10. Write them out and post them where you'll see them daily.

- Serve intentionally this week—look for a specific opportunity to bear someone's burden, show mercy, or encourage a believer in their race.

- Reevaluate your daily routines: Are you doing even mundane tasks for God's glory (1 Corinthians 10:31)? Invite Him into the ordinary.

- Obey the Great Commission: Share the Gospel with one person this week. Pray for boldness and clarity.

- Reignite a neglected spiritual discipline—perhaps Bible study, journaling, or worship—devote it to deepening your walk.

Prayer Prompts

- Father, thank You that I was not an accident or afterthought, but lovingly designed for Your glory.

- Jesus, help me walk in the good works You prepared for me—lead me daily in obedience and joy.

- Holy Spirit, remind me that my life is not my own. Empower me to live for the Kingdom, not for applause or comfort.

- Lord, I surrender my gifts, my story, my days, and my future. Use it all to draw others to You.

Journaling Space

Write from your heart. Consider using these prompts:

- What stood out most to you from this poem and Scripture set?

- How has God specifically revealed His purpose for your life recently?

- What calling or conviction is stirring in your spirit right now?

- What would it look like for you to finish this life faithful to His mission?

Mark Richard

Created for His glory—His own, not ours,
To shine like the stars, transformed by His powers.

Let this line fuel your daily walk.

4

THERE'S MERCY YET

A call to recognize the glory of God
through creation, conscience,
and Christ

BY MARK RICHARD

You can say there's no God—
But lift up your eyes.
Who painted the heavens,
Who carpeted the skies?

Who told the oceans, "Here you may tread,"
And carved out the mountains, their lofty bed?
Who placed the stars and named each one,
Then lit the world with fire and sun?

The heavens declare—have you not heard?
Creation speaks without a word.
From morning's light to midnight's dome,
The voice of God is plainly shown.

The wind that dances, the eagle's flight,
The hush of dusk, the roar of night.

Each breath you take, each beat you feel—
Is God revealing: I am real.

He sealed your hand with unseen art
And planted eternity in your heart.
You chase, you long, you seek, you strive—
For more than just this fleeting life.

Yet still you say, "There is no God,"
But Scripture calls your words as flawed.
The fool has said within his soul,
"No God for me—I'm in control."

But Truth's not swayed by man's debate—
God's presence does not fluctuate.
For from the first, He *was* and *is,*
The Maker of all that ever lives.

His power, His nature, His unseen hand—
Are clearly seen across the land.
No speech, no tongue can mute His voice—
You're not without, excuse or choice.

The sky won't plead,
The stones won't cry,
The time will pass,
The Judge will try.

So while there's breath—
O soul, be wise.
The God you mock
Still hears your cries.

Turn while you can today, repent,
To Jesus Christ whose heaven-sent.
He bore your sin, He paid your debt,
So even now—there's mercy yet.

POEM BASED ON THESE SCRIPTURES

All Scripture references are from the New King James Version (NKJV).

Genesis 1:1
In the beginning God created the heavens and the earth.

Psalms 19:1–6
The heavens declare the glory of God; and the firmament shows His handiwork... Day unto day utters speech, and night unto night reveals knowledge... Their line has gone out through all the earth...

Job 37:7
He seals the hand of every man, that all men may know His work.

Ecclesiastes 3:11
He has made everything beautiful in its time. Also He has put eternity in their hearts...

Psalms 14:1a
The fool has said in his heart, "There is no God."

Romans 1:20
For since the creation of the world His invisible attributes are clearly seen... so that they are without excuse.

REFLECTION & DEVOTIONAL PROMPTS

Heart Questions

- Do I truly see the hand of God in creation, or have I grown numb to its beauty and testimony?

- Have I ever questioned God's existence? If so, how did He draw me back to Truth?

- How do I respond to those who deny God—defensively, dismissively, or with compassion and boldness?

- What has God placed in my own heart that proves He is real—what longings, moments, or revelations?

- If I knew an unbelieving friend had only one chance to hear Truth, how would I tell them about Christ?

Action Steps

- Creation Meditation: Spend 15 minutes in quiet outside. Look at the sky, listen to nature, and reflect on Psalm 19. Write down what God shows you.

- Testify Boldly: Share this poem with a friend or family member who doubts God. Use it as a gentle invitation to dialogue.

- Pray by Name: List 2–3 people who have said, "there is no God." Pray daily for their heart to soften and eyes be opened.

- Keep Your Eyes Open: Start a gratitude list of ways you've seen God's invisible attributes in your daily life—nature, beauty, provision, conscience, love.

- Memorize Romans 1:20 or Psalm 14:1 to strengthen your evangelism and apologetics.

Prayer Prompts

- Creator God, open my eyes again to Your glory all around me—teach me to see and proclaim Your handiwork.

- Father, have mercy on those who deny You. Shine Your truth into their hearts. Help me be a vessel of love and boldness.

- Jesus, thank You that while we mock and run, You still invite us to repent and be saved.

- Holy Spirit, embolden me to speak truth in love—to never shrink back from defending the gospel, even to a scoffing world.

Journaling Space

Write and reflect from the heart:

- When was the last time creation stopped you in your tracks? What did it reveal to you about God?

- Who do you know that needs this truth most? What's your prayer for them?

- Where would I be if Jesus hadn't shown me mercy? How has He revealed Himself to me personally?

- Write your own praise: "Thank You, Lord, for revealing Yourself through…"

Turn while you can today, repent,
To Jesus Christ whose heaven-sent.
He bore your sin, He paid your debt,
So even now—there's mercy yet.

5

SALVATION'S CALL

An invitation to receive Christ,
examine your heart, and walk forward
in a new life

By Mark Richard

All have sinned, each soul gone wrong,
We've missed the mark, we don't belong.
We've chased the dark, ignored the Light,
Yet still God yearns to make us right.

The wages earned? A fatal breath,
Sin's final payment—eternal death.
But oh, the gift of love divine,
Eternal life in Christ is mine.

For God so loved this broken sphere,
He sent His Son to draw us near.
Not to condemn, but to redeem,
To take our guilt, to heal, to clean.

He wore our sin upon His frame,
The spotless Lamb, who bore our shame.

He took the nails, endured the tree,
So we might walk in victory.

Wounded for our transgressions deep,
Bruised for the secrets that we keep.
The stripes He bore—our healing won,
The wrath of God fell on the Son.

We all like sheep have lost our way,
Each chasing self, each gone astray.
But Christ, the Shepherd, took the blow,
To save our souls from death below.

And now He stands with arms stretched wide,
A risen King, the Crucified.
He calls, "Deny yourself—come near,
Take up your cross, and persevere."

Confess my Name, believe and live,
For Christ alone has power to give—
Not just a life, but life anew,
A holy fire to carry you.

If you believe He rose again,
Salvation's yours, forgiveness then.
He'll wash you clean, He'll make you whole,
And place His Spirit in your soul.

So listen close, O wandering heart,
This is the day for your fresh start.
The Savior's voice is pleading still—
Say "Yes" to grace. Receive His will.

POEM BASED ON THESE SCRIPTURES

All Scripture references are from the New King James Version (NKJV).

Romans 3:23
For all have sinned and fall short of the glory of God.

Romans 6:23
For the wages of sin is death, but the gift of God is eternal life in Christ Jesus our Lord.

John 3:16–17
For God so loved the world that He gave His only begotten Son, that whoever believes in Him should not perish but have everlasting life.
For God did not send His Son into the world to condemn the world, but that the world through Him might be saved.

II Corinthians 5:21
For He made Him who knew no sin to be sin for us, that we might become the righteousness of God in Him.

Isaiah 53:5–6
But He was wounded for our transgressions, He was bruised for our iniquities;
The chastisement for our peace was upon Him, and by His stripes we are healed.
All we like sheep have gone astray; we have turned, every one, to his own way;

And the Lord has laid on Him the iniquity of us all.

Matthew 16:24
Then Jesus said to His disciples, 'If anyone desires to come after Me, let him deny himself, and take up his cross, and follow Me.'

Romans 10:9
If you confess with your mouth the Lord Jesus and believe in your heart that God has raised Him from the dead, you will be saved.

I John 4:15
Whoever confesses that Jesus is the Son of God, God abides in him, and he in God.

REFLECTION & DEVOTIONAL PROMPTS

Heart Questions

- Do I recognize my need for a Savior; have I truly grasped the weight of my sin?

- Have I received the free gift of salvation by faith in Jesus Christ?

- What lies or pride have kept me from surrendering fully to God?

- Do I believe that God's grace is enough to wash me clean—no matter my past?

- If I have been saved, am I daily taking up my cross and following Jesus?

Action Steps

- Receive: If you've never surrendered your life to Jesus, today is the day of salvation. Confess your sins, believe He died and rose again, and invite Him into your heart.

- Repent and Return: If you've strayed, confess your sins and return to the cross. God's arms are still open wide.

- Profess and Memorize Salvation Truths: Commit Romans 10:9 and John 3:16 to memory. Speak them daily as your declaration of faith.

- Share the Gospel: Ask God to give you someone to share this message with. Salvation is too precious to keep to yourself.

- Follow Through in Faith: Take the next step—join a Bible-teaching church, be baptized, and get discipled.

Prayer Prompts

- Lord Jesus, I confess I have sinned and fallen short. I believe You died for me and rose again. Save me, cleanse me, and make me new.

- Father, thank You for the gift of salvation. Help me walk in it with confidence, humility, and boldness.

- Holy Spirit, remind me daily of who I am in Christ. Let the cross never grow dim to my heart.

- God, show me how to live a life that reflects the wonder of Your grace. May my life declare Your Gospel.

Journaling Space

- What sin or shame do I need to lay at the foot of the cross today?

- How has God shown me His love even while I was still running from Him?

- Write your personal salvation story:

- When did I truly receive Jesus as Lord? What changed in my life after that?

- Compose a personal declaration of faith:

- "I believe Jesus Christ is the Son of God. He died for me, rose again, and now lives in me. I am forgiven, free, and His forever."

Say 'Yes' to grace. Receive His will.

Now is the time to respond. Today is the day of salvation.

PART II:
WISDOM, IDENTITY, AND PRAYER

6

WHERE WISDOM BEGINS

A poetic reflection on holy fear that
leads to wisdom, safety, and
eternal life

BY MARK RICHARD

Before the mountains kissed the sky,
Before the stars began to fly,
He spoke—and all came into view,
The oceans deep, the morning dew.

The sun obeys His voice of light,
The galaxies proclaim His might,
And yet, He bends to hear our prayer—
This God who breathed the very air.

The fear of God—it starts right here,
Not trembling dread, but holy fear.
A sacred awe, a soul bowed low,
Before the One all heavens know.

"The fear of the Lord is wisdom's gate,"
Said Job, who stood beneath its weight.

To turn from evil, shun the snare,
Is understanding wrapped in prayer.

To fear the Lord is to begin—
A life that's free from death and sin.
The fool rejects instruction's call,
But wisdom lifts the humble tall.

"Come, simple ones!" the Spirit cries,
"Turn at My words, and lift your eyes.
I'll pour My Spirit from above,
And teach you truth and holy love."

It adds long days, it keeps us whole,
It quiets storms within the soul.
It teaches men to guard their way—
To walk with God both night and day.

It's better than the richest hoard,
This reverence for the sovereign Lord.
For treasures fade and bring distress,
But fearing God brings peace and rest.

The fear of God's a refuge sure,
A holy path that will endure.
It keeps us safe, it makes us wise—
It lifts our hearts, it clears our eyes.

And when life's final breath is drawn,
And judgment lights the breaking dawn,
Let this be said: "He walked with awe,
He feared his God, obeyed His law."

So seek Him now with treasure's fire,
Let wisdom be your heart's desire.
The fear of God is not the end—
It's only where true life begins.

POEM BASED ON THESE SCRIPTURES

All Scripture references are from the New King James Version (NKJV).

Job 28:28
And to man He said, "Behold, the fear of the Lord, that is wisdom, and to depart from evil is understanding."

Proverbs 1:7
The fear of the LORD is the beginning of knowledge, but fools despise wisdom and instruction.

I Peter 5:6
Therefore humble yourselves under the mighty hand of God, that He may exalt you in due time.

Proverbs 1:22–23
"How long, you simple ones, will you love simplicity? … Turn at my rebuke; Surely I will pour out My spirit on you…"

Proverbs 10:27
The fear of the LORD prolongs days, but the years of the wicked will be shortened.

Proverbs 15:16
Better is a little with the fear of the LORD than great treasure with trouble.

Proverbs 29:25
The fear of man brings a snare, but whoever trusts in the LORD shall be safe.

Proverbs 9:10
The fear of the LORD is the beginning of wisdom, and the knowledge of the Holy One is understanding.

Ecclesiastes 12:13–14
Fear God and keep His commandments, for this is man's all. For God will bring every work into judgment...

Proverbs 2:3–4
Yes, if you cry out for discernment, and lift up your voice for understanding, if you seek her as silver... you will understand the fear of the LORD.

REFLECTION & DEVOTIONAL PROMPTS

Heart Questions

- What comes to mind when you hear the phrase "fear of the Lord"? Do you see it as negative or life-giving?

- In what ways has reverence for God shaped your daily decisions, relationships, and values?

- Are you currently resisting or ignoring any instruction or correction from God?

- Do you prioritize wisdom like you would a hidden treasure (Proverbs 2:3–4)? Why or why not?

- Would those closest to you say you "walk in the fear of the Lord"? What evidence would they give?

Action Steps

- **Reverence in Practice**: Begin each morning this week with a short prayer acknowledging God's holiness, sovereignty, and wisdom.

- **Search Proverbs:** Spend time each day reading one chapter of Proverbs and note every mention of "fear of the Lord." Write them down and reflect on their application.

- **Humility Check:** Ask the Lord to show you any pride or rebellion that's hindering His instruction. Then humble yourself under His mighty hand (1 Peter 5:6).

- **Treasure Wisdom:** Choose a wise believer or mentor you respect and ask them what it looks like to live a life of reverent fear and holy wisdom.

- **Share the Truth**: If you mentor or lead others, discuss Ecclesiastes 12:13–14 with them. Encourage a fear of God rooted in love, not dread.

Prayer Prompts

- Lord, teach me to fear You rightly—not with panic, but with reverent awe and obedient love.

- Jesus, help me turn from the foolishness of this world and walk the narrow path of wisdom and life.

- Holy Spirit, convict me when I treat God's Word lightly. Make my heart soft and teachable.

- Father, let it be said of me: "He feared God, obeyed His voice, and walked in holy awe."

Journaling Space

Use these questions to write honestly and reflectively:

- Where am I living with too little reverence or too much casualness in my walk with God?

- What instruction from God have I been ignoring or resisting?

- How do I define "wisdom"? Does it align with Scripture's definition?

- Write a declaration: "I choose the fear of the Lord because…

*The fear of God is not the end—
It's only where true life begins.*

7

THINK AGAIN, LET CHRIST DEFINE

A spiritual invitation to examine your thoughts, expose lies, and replace them with God's truth

BY MARK RICHARD

Your thoughts, dear soul, are not benign—
They shape your heart, your path, your mind.
For what you think becomes your view,
And what you speak turns what you do.

The enemy lurks in your mind's thin veil,
Planting whispers, lies, and schemes to derail.
He crafts false scripts with subtle art—
To bind your soul and blind your heart.

"You're not enough," he repeatedly lies,
"You'll never change, so just disguise."
He fuels your fears and inflames your pride,
He fans the wounds you've locked inside.

But God has spoken a better Word—
His Truth more solid than what you've heard.
You are beloved, redeemed, and known;
His Spirit dwells in you—you're not alone.

So guard your mind—stand firm, alert!
Don't dress old lies in sacred shirts.
Take every thought and make it kneel—
To Christ, who speaks what's God and real.

First expose the lie within—
That voice of shame, that pull to sin.
Ask: Does this make me bold or scared?
Does it align with what God's declared?

If any bitterness or pride is near,
You've let a falsehood shape your fear.
But lies, once seen, lose all their bite
When we bring them to the Spirit's light.

Next replace with Truth divine—
From pages holy, strong, and fine.
Speak what God says over your days,
Scripture can reshape you in His ways.

"I am God's child—fearfully made.
I walk in light; I'm not afraid.
I'm loved with love no foe can sever.
Nothing can separate from Him—ever."

Then declare with a bold decree,
The Truth that God speaks over me:
"I am enough in Christ alone.
I'm not ashamed; I'm called His own."

I'm more than flesh, more than the fight,
I'm walking now in His Spirit's light.
So think again, and think with care.
God's Word, not wounds, is what you wear.

Let not the enemy script your mind—
Let Jesus speak. Let Christ define.

POEM BASED ON THESE SCRIPTURES

All Scripture references are from the New King James Version (NKJV).

II Corinthians 10:5
…casting down arguments and every high thing that exalts itself against the knowledge of God, bringing every thought into captivity to the obedience of Christ.

Romans 12:2
And do not be conformed to this world, but be transformed by the renewing of your mind…

Romans 8:6
For to be carnally minded is death, but to be spiritually minded is life and peace.

John 8:32
And you shall know the truth, and the truth shall make you free.

Psalm 139:14
I will praise You, for I am fearfully and wonderfully made…

I John 3:1
Behold what manner of love the Father has bestowed on us, that we should be called children of God…

Romans 8:38–39
For I am persuaded that neither death nor life… shall be able to separate us from the love of God which is in Christ Jesus our Lord.

REFLECTION & DEVOTIONAL PROMPTS

Heart Questions

- What thoughts have I allowed to define me that do not align with God's Word?

- Am I discerning the source of my thoughts— are they from the Spirit, my flesh, or the enemy?

- How do I respond when shame, fear, or unworthiness whisper into my mind?

- What truths from Scripture do I need to speak over myself more regularly?

- Have I allowed past wounds to write the script for my life instead of God's Word?

Action Steps

- Identify the Lie: Write down any recurring negative thoughts. Then test them: do they align with God's Word or oppose it (2 Corinthians 10:5)?

- Replace with Truth: For every lie, write down a truth from Scripture—such as "I am fearfully and wonderfully made" or "Nothing can separate me from God's love."

- Renew Your Mind Daily: Start your mornings with one verse that declares your identity in Christ. Let that be your mental anchor for the day (Romans 12:2).

- Speak Life Out Loud: Declare over yourself aloud what God says is true. Faith is strengthened not just by reading but by hearing (Romans 10:17).

- Filter Your Inputs: Be intentional about the voices you allow into your mind—media, people, music. Does it stir truth or confusion?

Prayer Prompts

- Lord Jesus, renew my mind and help me think in alignment with Your Word. Cast out lies I've believed and fill me with truth.

- Father, reveal the thoughts I've accepted that have shaped fear, pride, or shame in my life.

- Holy Spirit, teach me to take captive every thought that doesn't honor Christ and submit it to You.

- Abba, thank You that I am not defined by my feelings or failures but by Your love and truth.

Journaling Space

Write and reflect from the heart:

- What's one lie I've believed about myself or God? What truth from Scripture counters it?

- What thought patterns or strongholds have the enemy used to keep me bound?

- How has God shown me I am loved, known, and never alone in the past?

- Write a personal declaration rooted in truth, for example:

    o Today, I take every thought captive. I am not what the enemy says—I am who Christ declares me to be.

So think again, and think with care.
God's Word, not wounds, is what you wear.

8

BELIEVE IN PRAYER

An invitation to pray with confidence,
surrender, and expectancy

BY MARK RICHARD

When you feel the weight of life press in,
And joy is faint, and strength is thin,
When questions arise and peace departs—
You're not alone—God hears your heart.

He bids you come, draw near, and speak,
With humble confidence, strong yet meek.
No mask, no script, just honest cries—
The God of mercy, He never lies.

With every fear and every care,
He calls you to His house of prayer.
Not as a servant, stiff with dread,
But as a child, by grace now led.

"Seek My face," He gently says,
So seek Him now—His Truth, His ways.
With thanksgiving, let your burdens go,

He already knows what you long to know.

And when you knock, believe He hears—
Through faith, He'll wipe away your tears.
His answers come—yes, no, not yet—
But He'll never once your needs forget.

So pray for wisdom, strength, and light,
For daily bread and holy sight.
He gives beyond what we can dream—
Abundantly more, a flowing stream.

When unbelief begins to grow,
Cry, "Lord, I believe!" because He knows.
His power works within our frame,
To glorify His holy name.

So let us come—expectant, bold, and true—
For He awaits in love for me and you.
Seek first His Kingdom, trust His plan,
On earth as in Heaven, I believe, amen.

POEM BASED ON THESE SCRIPTURES

All Scripture references are from the New King James Version (NKJV).

I John 5:14–15
Now this is the confidence that we have in Him, that if we ask anything according to His will, He hears us. And if we know that He hears us… we know that we have the petitions that we have asked of Him.

Hebrews 4:16
Let us therefore come boldly to the throne of grace, that we may obtain mercy and find grace to help in time of need.

Philippians 4:6
Be anxious for nothing, but in everything by prayer and supplication, with thanksgiving, let your requests be made known to God.

Psalm 27:8
When You said, "Seek My face," my heart said to You, "Your face, LORD, I will seek."

Mark 11:24
Therefore I say to you, whatever things you ask when you pray, believe that you receive them, and you will have them.

Ephesians 3:20–21
Now to Him who is able to do exceedingly abundantly above all that we ask or think, according to the power that works in us, to Him be glory...

Mark 9:24
Immediately the father of the child cried out and said with tears, "Lord, I believe; help my unbelief!"

Matthew 6:33–34
But seek first the kingdom of God and His righteousness, and all these things shall be added to you. Therefore do not worry about tomorrow...

Matthew 6:10, 13

Your kingdom come. Your will be done on earth as it is in heaven... For Yours is the kingdom and the power and the glory forever. Amen.

REFLECTION & DEVOTIONAL PROMPTS

Heart Questions

- Do you believe God hears you, or mostly that He hears "prayerful people"?

- What keeps you from coming boldly to the throne of grace—fear, shame, doubt, busyness, unbelief?

- When you pray, do you submit to God's will, or mainly seek your preferred outcome?

- How do you respond when God's answer is "no" or "not yet"? Does it weaken or deepen your trust?

- Where do you most need to pray, "Lord, I believe; help my unbelief"?

- Are your prayers shaped by God's Kingdom priorities (Matthew 6:10; 6:33), or by daily anxieties?

Action Steps

- Daily 5-Minute Approach: For the next week, take 5 minutes each morning to "come boldly" (Hebrews 4:16). Use: *Praise → Confess → Thank → Ask.*

- Pray Scripture: Choose one verse above (e.g., 1 John 5:14–15 or Psalm 27:8) and pray it back to God word-for-word, inserting your own requests.

- Worry-to-Prayer Swap: Each time worry rises, stop and pray Philippians 4:6—out loud if possible.

- Faith List: Write 3 requests that seem "beyond what you can ask or think" (Ephesians 3:20). Pray them daily for 30 days and watch how God works—in outcomes or in you.

- Kingdom First Audit: Review your prayer journal (or start one). Highlight requests that are self-focused vs. Kingdom-focused. Ask God to realign your priorities (Matthew 6:33).

Prayer Prompts

- Father, I come because You invited me. I bring my needs, my doubts, and my heart. Hear me as I pray.

- Lord Jesus, I believe—help my unbelief. Strengthen my faith when I cannot see the answer yet.

- Holy Spirit, teach me to pray in harmony with the Father's will so that I may ask in confidence.

- Your kingdom come, Your will be done—in my heart, my family, my church, and my world. Amen.

Journaling Space

- Use these prompts to guide your writing time with the Lord:

- What burdens do I need to lay at God's throne today? List them.

- Where have I seen God answer prayer in the past? Record testimonies and give thanks.

- Write a personal "I believe—help my unbelief" prayer. Be specific.

- What would change in my life if I truly lived Matthew 6:33—seeking God's Kingdom first?

So let us come—expectant, bold, and true—
For He awaits in love for me and you.

9

THANKS BE TO GOD!

A celebration of the transforming
power of faith-fueled gratitude
and worship

BY MARK RICHARD

Give thanks to the Lord, for He is always good!
His mercy endures forever—as only it ever could.
Not just a habit, or something polite,
But gratitude shifts the soul into light.

It calms the anxious; it quiets the storm,
It warms the heart as it rewires the norm.
It silences worry with heaven-born peace,
It fills up the soul with Spirit-sent ease.

"Enter His gates with thanksgiving," we're told,
With praises and songs, let God's goodness unfold.
When we stop and remember all that God has done,
Gratitude rises like the marvelous morning sun.

Gratitude renews the mind as it reclaims the night,
It gives rest to the soul and vision to our sight.

For science is discovering what God always knew—
That thankfulness heals and makes all things new.

"Call on His name," declares Psalm 105,
"Make known His works, for God is alive!"
He is our portion, our strength, and our song,
A heart full of thanks will never be wrong.

So be thankful in trials, give thanks in the pain,
Let your praise rise in a sweet, melodious refrain.
Thanks repels the darkness; it drives demons away,
It welcomes God's glory to saturate your day.

Thankfulness isn't ignoring the ache,
It's trusting God's hand for what He will make.
It's faith in the fire; it's hope in the test,
Declaring, "My Jesus, You know what is best!"

"Let the Word of Christ dwell richly in you,"
Sing psalms and hymns with hearts made anew.
For every good gift, His mercy, our breath—
Thanks be to God, who has ruled over death!

Give thanks in all things, both bitter and sweet,
Lay fully your burdens at the Savior's feet.
Gratitude grows where worship is sown,
And Christ is exalted on the heavenly throne.

So teach me, O Lord, to number my days,
To walk with a heart that's steady in praise.
For when I give thanks, my soul finds its place—
I rejoice in your mercy and undeserved grace.

May gratitude guide me, no matter the cost—
Through joy and through sorrow, through gain and
through loss.
And when my last breath on earth I do raise—
May it glorify God with thanksgiving and praise.

POEM BASED ON THESE SCRIPTURES

All Scripture references are from the New King James
Version (NKJV).

I Chronicles 16:34
Oh, give thanks to the LORD, for He is good! For His
mercy endures forever.

Psalm 136:1
Oh, give thanks to the LORD, for He is good! For His
mercy endures forever.

Philippians 4:6–7
Be anxious for nothing, but in everything by prayer and
supplication, with thanksgiving... and the peace of
God... will guard your hearts and minds...

Psalm 100:4
Enter into His gates with thanksgiving, and into His
courts with praise. Be thankful to Him, and bless His
name.

Psalm 105:1–3
Oh, give thanks to the LORD! Call upon His name; Make known His deeds… Sing to Him, sing psalms to Him…

James 1:16–18
Every good gift… is from above, and comes down from the Father of lights…

I Thessalonians 5:18
In everything give thanks; for this is the will of God in Christ Jesus for you.

Ephesians 5:20
Giving thanks always for all things to God the Father in the name of our Lord Jesus Christ.

Colossians 3:14–17
Let the peace of God rule… and be thankful… Let the word of Christ dwell in you richly… singing… giving thanks to God the Father through Him.

Psalm 119:105
Your word is a lamp to my feet and a light to my path.

Hebrews 12:28–29
…Let us have grace, by which we may serve God acceptably with reverence and godly fear. For our God is a consuming fire.

I Corinthians 15:57
But thanks be to God, who gives us the victory through our Lord Jesus Christ.

II Corinthians 9:15
Thanks be to God for His indescribable gift!

REFLECTION & DEVOTIONAL PROMPTS

Heart Questions

- How often do you stop and intentionally give thanks to God in your daily routine?

- When you face hardship or fear, is your first response worry, or worship?

- How has thankfulness changed your perspective in past seasons of pain or waiting?

- Do you view gratitude as spiritual warfare—an act that repels darkness and welcomes God's presence?

- What are three specific blessings from God you've overlooked lately that you can thank Him for now?

Action Steps

- Start a gratitude journal for the next 7 days. Write down at least 5 things each day that you are thankful for—big or small.

- Memorize I Thessalonians 5:18 and declare it over your heart in both joy and trial.

- Write a letter or message to someone who has blessed you, sharing how God used them in your life.

- Incorporate worship music into your mornings or evenings. Sing psalms or hymns aloud to shift your atmosphere to praise.

- When worry rises, pause and pray using Philippians 4:6–7, choosing thanksgiving over anxiety.

Prayer Prompts

- Lord, thank You for Your goodness and mercy that endure forever—even when I don't feel it.

- Jesus, I surrender my anxiety and complaints. Teach me to thank You in all things, even the hard ones.

- Holy Spirit, cultivate a grateful heart in me. Let my worship be loud in the storm and humble in the blessing.

- Father, remind me daily that every good gift comes from You. I give You glory and praise for it all!

Journaling Space

Use this space to pour out your heart:

- What moments of thankfulness changed your perspective in the past?

- Where is God asking you to praise Him even when life feels uncertain?

- What would it look like to make gratitude your default posture?

- Write a prayer of thanksgiving for God's mercy, faithfulness, and victory in your life.

For when I give thanks, my soul finds its place—
I rejoice in Your mercy and undeserved grace.

PART III:
STAND FIRM AND
DEFEND YOUR FAITH

10

LURED: THE WAR FOR YOUR SOUL

A call to resist the enemy's schemes
and stand firm in the victory of Christ

BY MARK RICHARD

The Prince of the Air is prowling again,
Whispering lies into the hearts of man.
He steals, he kills, he seeks to destroy—
Every soul, every truth, every ounce of joy.

He's dressed in glamour, gloss, and glow,
But underneath in waiting? Hell's pit below.
He lures with screens and sensual sights,
With cravings, clicks, and empty nights.

Behind his curtain—don't be deceived—
He poisons, too, what we eat and breathe.
He distorts the seed; he corrupts the cure;
He floods our bodies with things impure.

Mark Richard

The news, the schools, the deceptive ads,
He paints what's wicked to look like "fads."
"Be free," he says, "just gratify!"
But his freedom's bait, and his truth's a lie.

He lures us all to believe his ply:
We watch it, hear it;
Laugh at it, and buy.

We exalt it, abide in it,
Bow to it, and lie.

We chase it, try it,
Binge on it, and hide.

All we desire is all that is it:
We keep its wick trimmed, ready, and lit.
For sleep can't come without its dose,
All while the deceiver prepares death's post.

He feeds our shame with more disguise—
With pills, and pride, and alibis.
He offers us highs to kill the lows.
Beyond every thrill? Is a fatal blow.

Our hearts now bruised;
Our minds confused.
Our bodies too, broken;
God's Truth, misspoken.

But God—our Redeemer—is greater still;
He breaks the chains; He bends our will.
Where Satan schemes, the Savior stands—
With grace and love and healing hands.

Christ gives to us the abundant life,
To pull us from our sins and strife,
To make us holy and set apart,
To cleanse our minds and guard our heart.

So don't be lured like Eve of old,
By shiny things and lies retold.
Stand firm, dear Christian, and be aware—
The Holy Spirit dwells in there.

You are a temple, bought with grace;
You bear His name; you know His face.
So fight the lure. Refuse his lies.
You are more than a conqueror—lift high your eyes!

POEM BASED ON THESE SCRIPTURES

All Scripture references are from the New King James Version (NKJV).

Ephesians 2:2
In which you once walked according to the course of this world, according to the prince of the power of the air, the spirit who now works in the sons of disobedience.

John 10:10
The thief does not come except to steal, and to kill, and to destroy. I have come that they may have life, and that they may have it more abundantly.

I Peter 5:8

Be sober, be vigilant; because your adversary the devil walks about like a roaring lion, seeking whom he may devour.

Genesis 3:4–6

Then the serpent said to the woman, "You will not surely die..." So when the woman saw that the tree was good for food... she took of its fruit and ate.

Romans 12:2

And do not be conformed to this world, but be transformed by the renewing of your mind...

I Corinthians 6:19–20

Do you not know that your body is the temple of the Holy Spirit...? You were bought at a price; therefore glorify God in your body and in your spirit, which are God's.

Romans 8:37

Yet in all these things we are more than conquerors through Him who loved us.

REFLECTION & DEVOTIONAL PROMPTS

Heart Questions

- Where have you been "lured" by the patterns of this world—especially through media, habits, or culture?

- Have you believed the lie that certain sins or addictions will satisfy, even momentarily? What has been the cost?

- Do you realize the enemy's agenda is not just temptation but destruction (John 10:10)?

- How would your mindset shift if you truly believed your body is the temple of the Holy Spirit (1 Corinthians 6:19)?

- Are you resisting the enemy daily, or are there areas where you've surrendered ground? What's your next step toward freedom?

Action Steps

- Identify the Lures: Make a list of things that regularly draw your attention away from God's will—entertainment, distractions, temptations—and commit each to prayer and surrender.

- Renew Your Mind: Memorize and meditate on Romans 12:2. Write it down. Tape it on your mirror or phone screen.

- Reclaim Your Body: Ask God to reveal any way you've dishonored your body or mind. Confess it. Choose to glorify Him in that area moving forward.

- Walk in Truth: Replace Satan's lies with Scripture. For each temptation or accusation, find a biblical truth and speak it aloud daily.

- **Fight with Worship**: Create a worship playlist specifically for spiritual warfare. Let truth-filled songs fuel your stand for purity and truth.

Prayer Prompts

- Jesus, I repent for where I've followed the world's ways instead of Yours. Cleanse my mind and redirect my affections.

- Father, open my eyes to the enemy's lures. Strengthen me to resist and stand firm in Your power.

- Holy Spirit, dwell in me fully—remind me that I am a temple, bought with a price. Help me live like I belong to You.

- Lord, thank You that I am more than a conqueror through Christ. Fill me with courage to fight the good fight of faith.

Journaling Space

Write your reflections to the Lord:

- Where am I most vulnerable to the enemy's lure?

- What lie has Satan been whispering to me lately? What truth from Scripture refutes it?

- How has God already shown me mercy, deliverance, or victory in the face of temptation?

- Declare: "Today I refuse the lure. I am not for sale—I am bought with the blood of Christ."

So fight the lure. Refuse his lies.
You are more than a conqueror—lift high your eyes!

11

SACRED SEXUALITY: GOD MADE US FOR ETERNITY

A Spirit-led call to holiness,
wholeness, and truth in a sexually
broken world

BY MARK RICHARD

Not to restrain, but to restore—
God's design is so much more
Than fleeting lust or passion's flame,
It's sacred Truth in Jesus' name.

Man and woman, God made them whole,
Each body He fashioned with a soul.
One man, one woman, joined for life—
In holy covenant, not fleeting strife.

This is the truth Christ came to show:
That hearts unguarded soon will go
Where lust gives birth to sin's decay,
And joy and peace are swept away.

"If your right eye leads you astray,
Pluck it out," Christ did say.
Not to shame or beat you down,
To trade earth's grief for Heaven's crown.

For from man's heart, all sins arise—
Adulteries and its shameful disguise.
Fornications and lusts untrue—
God sees the root inside of you.

The lust of flesh, the pride of life,
Distort what's sacred, pure, and right.
But in His will—our sanctity—
To walk in sacred sexuality.

The world will praise what God calls vile,
Glamorizing it, for a time or a while.
But every counterfeit we choose
Leads not to life—but to abuse.

Porn, perversion, self-gratifying acts—
They're chains that hold, not holy pacts.
God's standard isn't hate or shame—
It's holy love, a higher name.

No union He has ever blessed
Between two men, though culture pressed.
No sacred seal on same-sex pride,
We have His grace, if we abide.

His righteous path is narrow still,
Yet paved in joy and rich goodwill.
To walk with Christ in Truth and grace,
We flee the sin, and seek His face.

So single one—walk not in shame,
But celibate and uphold His name.
And married ones—stay true and whole,
Your bodies one, your hearts and soul.

And all who've sinned—there's still a way:
Be washed, be cleansed, redeemed today.
For such were some, but not still so—
When Jesus' blood begins to flow.

To follow Christ is not halfway—
It's *all* your heart, your night, your day.
Your mind, your body, and your soul—
In Him alone, you are made whole.

Deny yourself, take up your cross,
Count all things gain that once were loss.
Your sexuality's not your own—
It's His, and His design alone.

So trust in Him and not your eyes,
For fleeting pleasure only lies.
But those who walk the narrow path
Will know His love, escape His wrath.

God's sacred sexuality—
Not bondage, but serenity.
Not loss, but life eternally.
Not shame, but holy dignity.

Let every thought and act align
With Heaven's heart, with truth divine.
O Bride of Christ, arise and see:
God made you for eternity.

POEM BASED ON THESE SCRIPTURES

All Scripture references are from the New King James Version (NKJV).

Matthew 5:27–30
You have heard… 'You shall not commit adultery.' But I say to you that whoever looks at a woman to lust for her… has already committed adultery… If your right eye causes you to sin, pluck it out…

Matthew 15:19–20
Out of the heart proceed evil thoughts, murders, adulteries, fornications… These are the things which defile a man…

I John 2:15–17
Do not love the world… For all that is in the world—the lust of the flesh, the lust of the eyes, and the pride of life—is not of the Father…

I Thessalonians 4:3
For this is the will of God, your sanctification: that you should abstain from sexual immorality.

Hebrews 13:4
Marriage is honorable among all, and the bed undefiled; but fornicators and adulterers God will judge.

I Corinthians 6:9–11
Do not be deceived: neither fornicators… nor adulterers, nor homosexuals… will inherit the kingdom

90

of God. And such were some of you. But you were washed...

Matthew 19:4–6

"Have you not read that He who made them... made them male and female... and the two shall become one flesh... what God has joined together, let not man separate."

Genesis 1:27

So God created man in His own image... male and female He created them.

Genesis 2:24

Therefore a man shall leave his father and mother and be joined to his wife, and they shall become one flesh.

Matthew 7:13–14

Enter by the narrow gate... Because narrow is the gate and difficult is the way which leads to life...

Romans 1:26–27

For this reason God gave them up to vile passions... men with men committing what is shameful...

I Peter 1:15–16

Be holy in all your conduct... for it is written, "Be holy, for I am holy."

Galatians 5:19–21

The works of the flesh are evident... adultery, fornication, uncleanness... those who practice such things will not inherit the kingdom of God.

Matthew 22:37
You shall love the Lord your God with all your heart, with all your soul, and with all your mind.

Matthew 16:24–26
"If anyone desires to come after Me, let him deny himself, and take up his cross, and follow Me…"

Proverbs 3:5–6
Trust in the LORD with all your heart, and lean not on your own understanding…

Proverbs 3:7–8
Do not be wise in your own eyes; fear the LORD and depart from evil. It will be health to your flesh…

REFLECTION & DEVOTIONAL PROMPTS

Heart Questions

- Do you view God's design for sexuality as restrictive or redemptive? Why?

- Where have you believed cultural lies about identity, love, or sexual "freedom"?

- Have you personally experienced the consequences of sexual sin—emotionally, spiritually, or relationally? How has God brought or begun restoration?

- What does it mean to you that your sexuality is not your own—but God's design alone?

- How can you live set apart in a culture that praises what God calls sin?

Action Steps

- Repent and return: Confess any area of sexual compromise (past or present) to the Lord. Ask Him to cleanse and restore (1 Corinthians 6:11).

- Pursue purity: Whether single or married, create new boundaries to honor God with your thoughts, eyes, and body.

- Renew your mind: Meditate daily on Romans 12:1–2 and Proverbs 3:5–8. Let His Word reshape your thinking.

- Share your story: If God has delivered you from sexual sin or confusion, pray about how you can share your testimony to help others walk in freedom.

- Honor marriage: If married, renew your commitment to sacred sexuality within covenant love. If single, walk in celibacy as worship.

Prayer Prompts

- Father, thank You that Your design for sexuality is holy, healing, and full of life.

- Jesus, cleanse me from every impurity—whether seen, remembered, or hidden. Wash me in Your blood.

- Holy Spirit, help me walk the narrow path—not just with behavior, but with a heart fully surrendered.

- Lord, teach me to love what You love and reject what You call sin, even when it costs me.

Journaling Space

Use these prompts to write and reflect:

- Where do I need healing, freedom, or clarity when it comes to sexuality or identity?

- What does it look like to fully "deny myself, take up my cross, and follow Jesus" in this area?

- How have I seen God's design lead to peace, protection, or healing in my life or others'?

- Write a declaration of commitment: "I will honor God with my body, my desires, and my relationships…"

> *God's sacred sexuality—*
> *Not bondage, but serenity.*
> *Not loss, but life eternally.*
> *Not shame, but holy dignity.*

12

HOLY HEIRS

A pastoral call to live worthy of our
inheritance by imitating God in purity,
love, and righteousness

BY MARK RICHARD

No longer a slave, no longer bound—
A son, an heir—redemption found.
Within the Spirit cries, "Abba, Father,"
We rise in grace, looking no farther.

Let Christ's divine Word dwell deep inside,
In psalms and songs our hearts abide.
Flee every lure that tempts the flesh,
And run the race of righteousness.

Pursue what's godly, good, and pure,
In faith and love that shall endure.
With patience, gentleness as your guide,
Hold fast the Truth, let Christ abide.

Exercise your spirit every day,
Reject what's false—walk in His way.

Approve what's excellent and always right,
And shine with love, sincere, and bright.

Let not one word corrupt your lips,
But grace be found in all your scripts.
Let wrath and rage be cast aside,
With all offense and wounded pride.

Be kind and tenderhearted still,
Forgive as Christ forgave—His will.
Let mercy flow where anger stood,
And overcome wrong with every good.

For we are called to wear His name,
To live apart, not be the same.
To walk in Truth where few have trod,
As holy heirs, let us imitate God.

POEM BASED ON THESE SCRIPTURES

All Scripture references are from the New King James Version (NKJV).

Galatians 4:6–7
And because you are sons, God has sent forth the Spirit of His Son into your hearts, crying out, "Abba, Father!" Therefore you are no longer a slave but a son, and if a son, then an heir of God through Christ.

Colossians 3:16
Let the word of Christ dwell in you richly... teaching and admonishing one another in psalms and hymns... singing with grace in your hearts to the Lord.

I Timothy 6:11–14
But you... flee these things and pursue righteousness, godliness, faith, love, patience, gentleness... Fight the good fight... keep this commandment without spot, blameless until our Lord Jesus Christ's appearing.

I Timothy 4:7, 9–10
Reject profane and old wives' fables, and exercise yourself toward godliness... For to this end we both labor... because we trust in the living God...

Philippians 1:9–10
That your love may abound... that you may approve the things that are excellent... that you may be sincere and without offense...

Ephesians 4:29–32
Let no corrupt word proceed out of your mouth... Let all bitterness, wrath, anger... be put away... Be kind... tenderhearted... forgiving one another, even as God in Christ forgave you.

Ephesians 5:1
Therefore be imitators of God as dear children.

REFLECTION & DEVOTIONAL PROMPTS

Heart Questions

- Do I live each day with the awareness that I am a child and heir of God through Christ?

- In what areas of my life do I still act more like a slave to sin than a child of the King?

- What words or attitudes am I allowing that grieve the Holy Spirit (Ephesians 4:30–31)?

- Am I pursuing righteousness and godliness, or coasting spiritually?

- Do I imitate God's character in how I speak, love, forgive, and lead? Where am I falling short?

Action Steps

- Speak Like an Heir: Evaluate your words this week. Ask God to help you speak only what builds others up (Ephesians 4:29).

- Start Each Day with "Abba": Begin your prayers by calling God "Abba, Father" to realign your identity.

- Spiritual Exercise Plan: Just as you might plan physical workouts, make time each day this week for godliness—through Scripture reading, confession, or worship (1 Timothy 4:7).

- Imitate to Transform: Pick one specific trait of Christ (e.g., gentleness, patience, mercy). Study it in Scripture and ask the Holy Spirit to form it in you.

- Forgive as You've Been Forgiven: Is there anyone you're holding a grudge against? Write down their name and pray Ephesians 4:32 over them today.

Prayer Prompts

- Abba Father, thank You for adopting me as Your child and calling me Your heir through Christ.

- Lord Jesus, help me pursue righteousness and not be entangled again by sin. Strengthen me to flee and to follow You.

- Holy Spirit, fill me with grace and power to speak words that bless, forgive those who wrong me, and live as light in this dark world.

- God, make me a true imitator of You. Let others see Your nature in how I live, love, and serve.

Journaling Space

Write and reflect with the Lord:

- Where am I living beneath my identity as a holy heir?

- What specific Scripture from this poem stirred conviction or encouragement in me today?

- What do I think it truly means to "imitate God"? How can I start doing that more intentionally?

- Write a declaration: "Because I am a child of God, I will live as…"

To walk in Truth where few have trod,
As holy heirs, let us imitate God.

13

THE GOSPEL THEY DON'T PREACH: WOLVES IN SHEPHERD'S ROBES

A call to discernment, boldness, and
fidelity to God's true Gospel in a time
of false shepherds

BY MARK RICHARD

Woe to those who twist God's Truth—
Who preach with polish, but poison the youth.
They smile like shepherds, but devour like wolves,
Exalting their game, while God's Word dissolves.

Serving up rebellion in Jesus' Name.
They call evil good, yet good they shame,
They teach man's ideas as holy decree,
But their gospel is dead—it does not set free.

They come in sheep's clothing, with flattery and
charm,
But under their robes is the serpent's harm.
With swelling words and worldly gains,

Mark Richard

They promise freedom—but bind in chains.

They are lovers of self, and slaves to desire,
Liars destined for brimstone and fire.
Their doctrines darken what once was right.
They serve their belly, not the Lord of Light,

Let them be accursed—so says the Word,
For they've twisted the Truth that once they heard.
It would've been better if they had never known
Than to trample the blood at the foot of the throne.

And yet, beloved, be not deceived—
The Gospel of Christ must still be believed.
Guard your heart, and test each voice:
For only one Truth leads to righteous choice.

Mark and avoid them—do not be swayed,
By the softest voice or the smoothest blade.
If they do not speak in line with God's Word,
Then their counsel is dead, and their wisdom absurd.

The time has come, both watch and warn—
The Bride of Christ must not be torn.
Call out the wolves, expose the lies,
Stand firm in truth—the hour is nigh.

POEM BASED ON THESE SCRIPTURES

All Scripture references are from the New King James Version (NKJV).

Isaiah 5:20–21
Woe to those who call evil good, and good evil;
Who put darkness for light, and light for darkness;
Who put bitter for sweet, and sweet for bitter!
Woe to those who are wise in their own eyes,
And prudent in their own sight!

Hosea 4:6
My people are destroyed for lack of knowledge.
Because you have rejected knowledge, I also will reject you from being priest for Me;
Because you have forgotten the law of your God, I also will forget your children.

Matthew 7:15
Beware of false prophets, who come to you in sheep's clothing, but inwardly they are ravenous wolves.

Mark 7:7
And in vain they worship Me, Teaching as doctrines the commandments of men.

II Peter 2:1–3
But there were also false prophets among the people, even as there will be false teachers among you,
who will secretly bring in destructive heresies, even denying the Lord who bought them, and bring on

themselves swift destruction. And many will follow their destructive ways, because of whom the way of truth will be blasphemed. By covetousness they will exploit you with deceptive words; for a long time their judgment has not been idle, and their destruction does not slumber.

II Peter 2:18–21

For when they speak great swelling words of emptiness, they allure through the lusts of the flesh...

While they promise them liberty, they themselves are slaves of corruption... It would have been better for them not to have known the way of righteousness, than having known it, to turn from the holy commandment delivered to them.

Galatians 1:9–10

As we have said before, so now I say again, if anyone preaches any other gospel to you than what you have received, let him be accursed. For do I now persuade men, or God? Or do I seek to please men? For if I still pleased men, I would not be a bondservant of Christ.

Romans 16:17–18

Now I urge you, brethren, note those who cause divisions and offenses, contrary to the doctrine which you learned, and avoid them. For those who are such do not serve our Lord Jesus Christ, but their own belly, and by smooth words and flattering speech deceive the hearts of the simple.

Revelation 21:8

But the cowardly, unbelieving, abominable, murderers, sexually immoral, sorcerers, idolaters, and all liars shall have their part in the lake which burns with fire and brimstone, which is the second death.

REFLECTION & DEVOTIONAL PROMPTS

Discernment Questions

- Am I spiritually discerning the messages I receive—even if they come from popular or polished voices?

- Do I weigh every teaching against the full counsel of God's Word, or do I rely on feelings and flattery?

- Are there "false gospels" I've allowed to creep into my beliefs—messages that please man but betray Christ?

- Have I lacked courage to speak the truth because it might offend, divide, or cost me influence?

Action Steps

- Test Everything (I Thessalonians 5:21): Compare all sermons, songs, and "Christian" content to Scripture.

- Name the Lie: Write down a modern false teaching you've encountered (e.g., love without holiness, self as center). Then replace it with God's Truth.

- Be Bold in Love: When needed, lovingly expose error and point people back to Jesus' Word, not opinion.

- Uplift True Teachers: Encourage pastors and leaders who preach the full Gospel with truth and grace.

- Clean Your Feed: Remove influence from teachers, accounts, or books that water down, distort, or twist God's truth.

Prayer Prompts

- Father, give me the eyes to discern and the courage to speak. Let me not be deceived, but walk in your whole truth.

- Lord Jesus, protect Your Bride from wolves in robes. Raise up shepherds who preach Christ crucified—nothing more, nothing less.

- Holy Spirit, purify my own heart. May I never seek to please man over You. Burn away all that's not of You.

- God, help me contend for the faith once delivered and never shrink back. Let truth and love guide me in equal measure.

Journaling Space

- Record a time when you were exposed to a false or incomplete gospel.

- How did it feel? What helped you see the truth?

- Write a declaration of faithfulness, for example:

  o "I will not compromise. I will stand firm on the unchanging Word of God, even when others distort it."

- Reflect on this:

  o How can I be part of the remnant that guards the flock and lifts up Christ, the True Shepherd?

The Bride of Christ must not be torn...

PART IV:
WARNINGS AND A CALL TO ACTION

14

WHERE THE FIRE IS NEVER QUENCHED

A solemn warning about the eternal
consequences of rejecting Christ

BY MARK RICHARD

They scoff and smirk and laugh out loud,
Joke of flames beneath the ground.
As if the Judge, so just and true,
Would wink at sin and let it through.

But hell is real—it burns, it waits,
For every soul who seals their fate.
Not by God's cruel hand, per se,
But by rejecting Christ—the only Way.

It's not a party; it's not a game,
Not firelight with friends and flame.
It's torment deep, it's weeping sore,
It's knowing Truth, forevermore.

Jesus warned with words so dire:
Of "hellfire" and "quenchless fire."

Better to lose a limb, or an eye,
Than be whole in sin and cursed to die.

In Hades' flame, the rich man cried,
While poor men soared to heaven's side.
A chasm wide, no bridge to span—
No second chance for fallen man.

Eternal ruin, no reprieve,
No hope, no light, no sweet relief.
Just wrath, just loss, just deep regret—
A soul condemned who won't forget.

And yet they live as if immune,
As if the Judge delays too soon.
But Sodom's fire—an ancient cry—
Still warns the world how sinners die.

The Lamb once slain holds every key,
To Hades, death, and destiny.
The Book of Life will tell it all—
Whose name is there, and who will fall.

The second death, the fiery sea,
Awaits the proud, faithless, and cowardly.
The idol hearts, the hands that kill,
The liars who reject God's will.

But you, dear soul—take heed today.
The cross still speaks, the Spirit prays.
While breath remains, while mercy calls,
Repent! Believe—before you fall.

For hell is real, and time is brief.
Don't trade your soul for lies or grief.
Narrow is the path that leads to life.
Run to the Savior—escape death's strife.

POEM BASED ON THESE SCRIPTURES

All Scripture references are from the New King James Version (NKJV).

Psalm 9:17
The wicked shall be turned into hell, and all the nations that forget God.

Matthew 25:46
And these will go away into everlasting punishment, but the righteous into eternal life.

Matthew 10:28
And do not fear those who kill the body but cannot kill the soul. But rather fear Him who is able to destroy both soul and body in hell.

Matthew 18:8–9
If your hand or foot causes you to sin, cut it off... It is better... than having two hands or two feet, to be cast into the everlasting fire... rather than... to be cast into hell fire.

Mark 9:43

If your hand causes you to sin, cut it off. It is better for
you to enter into life maimed, than... to go to hell, into
the fire that shall never be quenched—

Luke 16:22–26

...The beggar died and was carried... to Abraham's
bosom... the rich man also died... and being in
torments in Hades... cried... "I am tormented in this
flame." ...Between us and you there is a great gulf
fixed...

II Thessalonians 1:9

These shall be punished with everlasting destruction
from the presence of the Lord and from the glory of
His power.

Jude 7

...Sodom and Gomorrah... are set forth as an
example, suffering the vengeance of eternal fire.

Revelation 1:18

I am He who lives, and was dead, and behold, I am alive
forevermore. Amen. And I have the keys of Hades and
of Death.

Revelation 20:13–15

...And they were judged, each one according to his
works. Then Death and Hades were cast into the lake
of fire... Anyone not found written in the Book of Life
was cast into the lake of fire.

Revelation 21:8
But the cowardly, unbelieving… and all liars shall have their part in the lake which burns with fire and brimstone, which is the second death.

REFLECTION QUESTIONS & DEVOTIONAL PROMPTS

Heart Questions

- Do you truly believe in the reality of hell as Jesus described it, or have you dismissed or minimized it in your heart or teaching?

- What would it mean for your life, priorities, and relationships if you lived with eternity in view every day?

- Are there people in your life who need to hear this truth, but you've been hesitant to speak it? Why?

- Is your name written in the Book of Life? Have you repented, believed in Christ, and surrendered fully to Him?

- Do you treat sin lightly, or do you fear God and flee temptation, as Jesus urged in His teaching about hell?

Action Steps

- Take spiritual inventory: Examine your salvation. Have you trusted in Jesus alone for the forgiveness of your sins?

- Pray for boldness to share the Gospel with someone who is lost. Write their name down. Ask God for the right moment and words.

- Confess any sin you've tolerated or justified in your life. Remember: Jesus said it's better to lose what causes us to sin than to perish eternally.

- Write a letter or message to a loved one warning them compassionately about eternity, filled with Scripture and truth.

- Read Luke 16 aloud this week and meditate on the rich man's cry. Ask God to break your heart for the lost.

Prayer Prompts

- Lord, awaken my heart to the seriousness of sin and the reality of eternal separation from You.

- Jesus, thank You for warning us with love, clarity, and urgency. Help me respond with faith and holy fear.

- Holy Spirit, give me courage to speak the truth in love, even when it's uncomfortable or rejected.

- Father, have mercy on those I love who are far from You. Draw them to repentance while there is still time.

Journaling Space

- How did this poem impact you emotionally and spiritually?

- What did you feel God speaking to you through the warnings of Scripture?

- Who is God putting on your heart to intercede for or reach out to with the Gospel?

- Write a prayer of commitment to live with eternity in view.

Repent! Believe—before you fall.
For hell is real, and time is brief.
Don't trade your soul for lies or grief.

115

15

A THIEF IN THE NIGHT

A powerful reminder of Christ's
imminent return and a call for
believers to be sober, ready,
and faithful

BY MARK RICHARD

In the stillness of night and all seems right,
When laughter echoes and hearts feel light,
A soundless step, then a trumpet's blare—
The Son of Man will split the air.

Many say, "Peace and safety"—so sure, so blind,
But sudden destruction they'll surely find
Their hearts weighed down by worldly cares,
By drunken feasts and selfish snares.

Not with forewarning, nor a siren's test,
But sudden and sure—He'll come at last.
A thief in the night, no time to plead,
No time to barter, no time to heed.

Like the virgins who waited with lamps in hand,
Some were wise, prepared, and ready to stand.
But others slumbered, their oil ran dry—
And missed the Bridegroom passing by.

Cries rang out, "He's drawing near!"
But only the ready could really hear.
The door was shut; their cries too late—
A sobering silence sealed their fate.

Oh Church, awake! The hour is close!
The heavens stir, the trumpet boasts!
The sky will open—a radiant sight,
Christ rides in glory, clothed in white.

His eyes aflame, His justice sure,
His robe dipped red, forever pure.
With armies dressed in linen white,
He rides to claim His Bride this night.

So watch, and pray, please guard your soul,
Let no distraction take its toll.
Don't let your oil of faith run low—
Keep trimmed your lamp; be set to go.

For Christ will come—you know not when.
Will He find you chasing sin?
Or bowed in reverent, holy fear,
Awaiting Him to reappear?

Let not His voice be strange that day,
Let not His glory cast you away.
Be watchful, sober, and full of light,
For Jesus is coming, as a thief in the night.

POEM BASED ON THESE SCRIPTURES

All Scripture references are from the New King James Version (NKJV).

I Thessalonians 5:2–3
For you yourselves know perfectly that the day of the Lord so comes as a thief in the night.
For when they say, 'Peace and safety!' then sudden destruction comes upon them, as labor pains upon a pregnant woman. And they shall not escape.

Luke 21:34–36
But take heed to yourselves, lest your hearts be weighed down with carousing, drunkenness, and cares of this life, and that Day come on you unexpectedly.
For it will come as a snare on all those who dwell on the face of the whole earth.
Watch therefore, and pray always that you may be counted worthy to escape all these things that will come to pass, and to stand before the Son of Man.

Matthew 24:44
Therefore you also be ready, for the Son of Man is coming at an hour you do not expect.

Matthew 25:1–13 (The Parable of the Ten Virgins)
…And at midnight a cry was heard: 'Behold, the bridegroom is coming; go out to meet him!' …
And while they went to buy, the bridegroom came, and those who were ready went in with him…

And the door was shut... Watch therefore, for you know neither the day nor the hour in which the Son of Man is coming.

Mark 13:32–33
But of that day and hour no one knows, not even the angels in heaven, nor the Son, but only the Father. Take heed, watch and pray; for you do not know when the time is.

I Peter 4:7
But the end of all things is at hand; therefore be serious and watchful in your prayers.

Daniel 7:13
I was watching in the night visions, And behold, One like the Son of Man, Coming with the clouds of heaven! He came to the Ancient of Days, And they brought Him near before Him.

Revelation 19:11–16
Now I saw heaven opened, and behold, a white horse. And He who sat on him was called Faithful and True... clothed with a robe dipped in blood... And the armies in heaven... followed Him on white horses... King of Kings and Lord of Lords.

Revelation 22:20
He who testifies to these things, 'Surely I am coming quickly.' Amen. Even so, come, Lord Jesus!

REFLECTION QUESTIONS & DEVOTIONAL PROMPTS

Heart Questions

- If Jesus returned today, would He find me ready—or distracted by the world?

- Am I storing up oil like the wise virgins—or letting my lamp run dry?

- Do I long for Christ's return—or secretly hope He delays so I can enjoy sin a bit longer?

- What worldly cares or habits are dulling my spiritual alertness?

- Have I grown lukewarm in prayer, purity, or purpose?

Action Steps

- Watch and Pray: Establish or renew a daily rhythm of prayer. Stay spiritually awake.

- Trim Your Lamp: Examine your faith. Repent of sin, rekindle your love for God, and keep your oil—your heart and spirit—filled with His Word.

- Live Set Apart: Declutter your life from distractions that hinder your readiness (e.g., music, movies, relationships, social media, addictions, apathy).

- Encourage Others: Gently remind other believers that Christ is returning. Don't let loved ones be unprepared.

- Anchor in Eternity: Live today in light of that glorious day. Let your decisions, dreams, and priorities reflect the soon return of the King.

Prayer Prompts

- Lord, awaken my soul. Let me not sleep through this spiritual hour. Make me watchful, sober, and prepared for Your return.

- Jesus, cleanse me from the distractions and desires of this world. Teach me to number my days and live in light of eternity.

- Holy Spirit, fill my lamp. Let my heart burn with longing for the Bridegroom. Keep me faithful and full of light.

- Come, Lord Jesus. Let me be found ready—blameless and waiting with joy when You split the skies.

Journaling Space

Write out a personal inventory:

- Am I living as if Jesus could return today?

- What areas of my life need repentance, preparation, or rededication?

- Reflect on a time when you were most spiritually awake.

- What habits or heart-postures were in place then that you may need to return to?

Record a declaration of readiness, for example:

- "Jesus, I want to be found faithful. I am watching and waiting. I will live today for Your glory and return."

Don't let your oil of faith run low—
Keep trimmed your lamp; be set to go.

16

LET YOUR LIFE PREACH

A call to be doers of the Word
and examples of Christ in a
watching world

BY MARK RICHARD

Don't just be hearers who nod and agree,
But doers of Truth for the whole world to see.
Let your life be a mirror of all Jesus taught—
In action, in kindness, in word, and in thought.

Do unto others as you would receive,
With hearts full of mercy, quick to believe.
Look out for your neighbor, not just for your own—
And sow seeds of love where coldness has grown.

Be swift to hear and slow to speak,
Let patience and gentleness crown the meek.
No harsh words or anger that tear apart—
But words that edify and soften the heart.

Be kind and tender, forgiving and true,
Just as Christ Jesus has forgiven you.

Let no corrupt talk escape your lips,
But grace and Truth on every trip.

A merry heart—like medicine sweet,
Can lift the fallen and strengthen the weak.
So dwell on what's noble, what's lovely and right,
Think thoughts of virtue, and walk in the light.

Comfort the weary, build up the low,
Encourage the faithful wherever you go.
Forget not to share or to bless with your hand—
Such offerings rise so sweet to the Lamb.

Let all be done in humility's name,
Not seeking position, praise, or fame.
Honor one another, love without end—
Be a peacemaker, brother, and a faithful friend.

Walk worthy of the call you received,
With gentleness shown and grace believed.
Let the Spirit bear fruit: joy, peace, and love—
Self-control, kindness—all from above.

Love suffers long, is patient and kind,
Not puffed up or selfish, but of a sound mind.
So do good to all, while you still may—
Especially to those who walk in the Way.

Have compassion, be courteous, bless, not revile,
You're called to inherit, so walk every mile.
Not just with your lips, but with hands and with
feet—
Let faith become action, with everyone you meet.

POEM BASED ON THESE SCRIPTURES

All Scripture references are from the New King James Version (NKJV).

James 1:22
But be doers of the word, and not hearers only, deceiving yourselves.

Luke 6:31
And just as you want men to do to you, you also do to them likewise.

Philippians 2:4
Let each of you look out not only for his own interests, but also for the interests of others.

James 1:19
So then, my beloved brethren, let every man be swift to hear, slow to speak, slow to wrath.

Ephesians 4:32
And be kind to one another, tenderhearted, forgiving one another, even as God in Christ forgave you.

Ephesians 4:29
Let no corrupt word proceed out of your mouth, but what is good for necessary edification, that it may impart grace to the hearers.

Proverbs 17:22
A merry heart does good, like medicine, But a broken spirit dries the bones.

Philippians 4:8
Whatever things are true... noble... just... pure... lovely... of good report... if there is any virtue and if there is anything praiseworthy—meditate on these things.

I Thessalonians 5:11
Therefore comfort each other and edify one another, just as you also are doing.

Hebrews 13:16
But do not forget to do good and to share, for with such sacrifices God is well pleased.

Philippians 2:3
Let nothing be done through selfish ambition or conceit, but in lowliness of mind let each esteem others better than himself.

Proverbs 27:2
Let another man praise you, and not your own mouth; A stranger, and not your own lips.

Romans 12:10
Be kindly affectionate to one another with brotherly love, in honor giving preference to one another;

Ephesians 4:1–3
Walk worthy of the calling… with all lowliness and gentleness, with longsuffering, bearing with one another in love…

Galatians 5:22–23
The fruit of the Spirit is love, joy, peace, longsuffering, kindness, goodness, faithfulness, gentleness, self-control…

I Corinthians 13:4
Love suffers long and is kind; love does not envy; love does not parade itself, is not puffed up…

Galatians 6:10
Therefore, as we have opportunity, let us do good to all, especially to those who are of the household of faith.

I Peter 3:8–9
…be of one mind, having compassion… love as brothers, be tenderhearted, be courteous… not returning evil for evil… but on the contrary blessing…

REFLECTION QUESTIONS & DEVOTIONAL PROMPTS

Heart Questions

- Does your daily life reflect the teachings of Jesus, or have you become more of a hearer than a doer?

- When people observe your conduct, are they drawn toward Christ? Why or why not?

- Which fruit(s) of the Spirit do you most need to grow in right now?

- Is there area where pride, anger, or selfish ambition is undermining your witness?

- Do you bless others with your speech, generosity, and presence, or are you more passive in your faith?

Action Steps

- Examine your week: Were your actions toward others Christ-like in tone, timing, and truth? Where might God be inviting you to repent and adjust?

- Practice Philippians 2:4 today—look out for someone else's needs above your own. Ask God to show you who and how.

- Choose one verse from this poem's Scripture list to memorize and live out with intention.

- Write down three ways you will let your life preach this week—in your home, work, and community.

- Speak a blessing this week over someone you might normally overlook or struggle to love (I Peter 3:9).

Prayer Prompts

- Lord, forgive me for the times I've agreed with Your Word but failed to live it out. Help me be a faithful doer.

- Holy Spirit, grow in me the fruit of gentleness, love, and self-control. Make me a witness who reflects Jesus well.

- Jesus, let my life preach louder than my words. May others see You in how I serve, speak, and respond.

- Father, teach me to walk humbly and joyfully in my calling, reflecting the grace that You've so freely given me.

Journaling Space

Use these questions to guide your time of writing:

- What line from the poem impacted you the most? Why?

- What is one way your life could better "preach" the Gospel?

- Where is God calling you to *do* something—not just *know* something?

- Record a prayer for someone you can bless or serve in action this week.

Not just with your lips, but with hands and
with feet—
Let faith become action, with everyone you meet.

CONNECT WITH ME

Thank you for reading *Words for a Wounded World.* My hope and prayer are that these poems, Scriptures, and reflection prompts have spoken to your heart, mind, and soul; challenged your thinking, or strengthened your relationship in Christ. I'd love to hear what specific poems, passages, and Scriptures spoke deeply to you.

Here's how you can connect:

Website: MarkRichardMinistry.com

Email: MarkRichardMinistry@gmail.com

Follow me on Facebook:
facebook.com/markrichardministry

Invite me to speak: If you'd like me to speak at your church, event, or group, please reach out through my website or email.

ABOUT THE AUTHOR

Mark Richard is a Christ-centered author and Bible teacher with a passion for proclaiming truth and grace in a confused and broken world. After leaving behind decades of a sexually sinful lifestyle to follow Jesus wholeheartedly, Mark now devotes his life to sharing the hope, healing, and freedom found only in God's Word.

Through Scripture-saturated writings, workshops, and publications, Mark equips believers to walk in holiness, speak truth with love, and live fully for Christ. His writing is deeply personal, theologically grounded, and driven by the belief that God's Word alone transforms hearts, minds, and lives.

Mark is the author of the upcoming book, ***Sacred Sexuality: Grace and Truth Revealed in a Culture of Confusion.*** He serves as a teacher for churches, small groups, and individuals seeking spiritual renewal. His writing has touched lives across generations, offering conviction, clarity, and comfort in a time of great need. Connect with him at: MarkRichardMinistry.com.

Words for a Wounded World *is* his first collection of Scripture-inspired poetry.

ABOUT KHARIS PUBLISHING:

Kharis Publishing, an imprint of Kharis Media LLC, is a leading Christian and inspirational book publisher based in Aurora, Chicago metropolitan area, Illinois. Kharis' dual mission is to give voice to under-represented writers (including women and first-time authors) and equip orphans in developing countries with literacy tools. That is why, for each book sold, the publisher channels some of the proceeds into providing books and computers for orphanages in developing countries so that these kids may learn to read, dream, and grow. For a limited time, Kharis Publishing is accepting unsolicited queries for nonfiction (Christian, self-help, memoirs, business, health and wellness) from qualified leaders, professionals, pastors, and ministers. Learn more at: https://kharispublishing.com/

www.ingramcontent.com/pod-product-compliance
Lightning Source LLC
LaVergne TN
LVHW061222211025
823911LV00006B/12